DIVINE

ANVESHA SAHDEO

Contents

THE BOOK 'DIVINE' IS A POETRY BASED BOOK WRITTEN BY POETESS ANVESHA SAHDEO. SHE WAS BORN IN A SMALL DISTRICT OF JHARKHAND, INDIA. HER FATHER NAME IS MR. LAL NATH VISHAL SAHDEO AND HER MOTHER IS MRS. VINITA SAHDEO. ANVESHA CULTIVATED HER WRITING SKILL AT A VERY TENDER AGE AND IS A YOUNG TEENAGE POETESS.

SHE IS THE YOUNGEST POETESS TO BE PUBLISHED BY NOTIONPRESS AT A AGE OF 15.

WE THANK HER FOR HER SUPPORT REGARDING US AND WE AS A TEAM CONGRATULATE HER FOR HER HAPPY WRITING JOURNEY.

Dear Me

Dear me! You re a temper,

Control it, you will get through.

But, do not over control it,

Because you will lose you.

Dear me! You're smile is lovely,

Keep it up even at all time

When you really can't, because,

You might lose it anytime!

Dear me! Never trust your friends!

They are the world, it appears.

But all friendships last no longer

Than a handful of years.

Dear me! You're strong and powerful.

You're a beast of strengths.

But remember you gain them

Only through life's breaths and lengths.

Express Yourself

I also want to see the world

I also want to see sunrise.

Sometimes also want to answer

Instead ofjust hidding aside

I also want to reach on the top

And once want to feel the pride.

Want to see my parentS priceless smile

While I get any prize.

But I am afraid to show myself

Just feel a little uncomfortable

Unable to express myself

to show the world how much I am capable

But for one thing I feel proud on me

That the only thing I hide is my

tiny little thaught.

I am atleast not like those I see

Roses from out and inside bushes of thorns.

The people who are big with money and wealth

But there thaughts are so small.

But I am one of those books

Which is open to all.

My Mother, My Strength

She wakes up Before

The Home Has Leisurely Stretched,

While the Morning Still to Brighten,

While the Night is Still to Leave.

She Has Already Prepared For the Next Day

Mom Was Granted The Powers of a God,

Time Slows down for Her

Food is Always Plentiful when Cooked By Her Hands

Not a Soul Left Hungry.

My Mother Was Granted Magic

As She Stepped onto Earth

But She Forsakes the Touch of Midas

For the Touch of Love, compassion & Motherhood.

I wish We Celebrate Her More,

The Heartbeat of the Household

the Most Unselfish that Love Can be,

the Purest that It Can Be,

The Most Cosseted Love is That Of Hers.

There is Music in Her Chortle

the Inchoate Laughter sounds

Like an Arpeggio, an Overture

To the Beautiful Sound of Her Happiness.

There is Something Magical about Her Smile,

There's No Better Sight

than to See Her Smile,

Her Happiness like an Air Balloon

for the Weights on My Shoulder,

That Ever Forgiving Unburdening Smile.

Rays Of Freedom

From the dusk to the dawn

From earth to the sky

From poor to the rich

One day the rays of freedom will Conqueror.

Oppressors will get oppressed

By the buds of the dark roses

The sky will again rain happyness

The blood of roses will kill away darkness.

The tears in eyes will dry out

The blood of matyers

The prayers of mothers

Will bear fruits for the oppressed.

The bloody nights,dark stars

Sky is bleeding holding the rain

Blood in seas, watering coffins

Hope one day rays will eross the terrain.

Papa, My Superhero

The God In disguise

The ephemeral viIbe

The hero in conscise

The unforgettable prize.

The house of power

The man of all weather

The summer in winter

The winter in surmmer.

The voice of dreams

The man who never screams

The maker of my creams

The originator of all beams.

The man who lead us to goal

The man who kept us as his soul

The man who patted in distress

The man who kept us safe while self in stress.

The man without world is a big zero

The ideal the superman my big hero

The man of encouragement and inspiration

The man who helped to gain recognition.

The man who can't be felicitated by a day

The man who be seen each day as sun ray

My dad My Superhero!

In Her Mind

What reincarnation was

She used to wonder

Travelling past was adventurous

That idea thrilled her.

She was deep into the land of fantasy

Used to imagine what life to be

The supernatural spirit's story

The secret behind night's glory.

The magic amazed her

She believed in miracle

The world beyond universe

Was used to be her imagination!

My Life

World is made of love,

And there is nothing above.

Nature is full of beauty,

And it's our prime duty.

Everyone left me,

But my heart assisted me.

I loved everyone from outside,

But everything was dull inside.

No one loved me,

But I was with me.

No one trusted me,

But I was with me.

So, today I am having fun

With no more feelings for anyone.

Like a fairy tale

I wished I had wings

Like a fairy in fairy tale

I wished I would fly high

Like a fairy in fairy tale.

I would have embrace

The world with love

I would been selfiess

And helping others.

Would have no fear

And could use super powers

Just like a fairy tale

World would have been magical.

Dreams

My Dreams aren't big,

But not even small

Ilive an independent life,

And that's it all!

1 go to my dream working space,

With a bag in my hands,

And,My head held high!

I wanna live my dream,

And just wanna fly!

I see countless inspiring women,

Doing best in their fields,

But also the talented women,

Who just only dreamed!

Both are my motivation

In numnerous ways,

I look up to them,

In my tough days.

I want to travel the world,

And reach to the sky.

I want to live in my own home,

And do not want to rely.

Maybe it's hard,

But I really want to try.

I wanna live my dreamn,

And just wanna fly!

Unknown Girl

A girl walking with ice in her heart

With questions in her mind

With water in her eyes

With pain that no one can see

She's as pure as the snow on the Himalayas,

And quiet just like the lake.

She's as bright as the moon

With a little yellowish shade.

Is she a ignored girl?

Who is filled with shame?

Or is she a silent girl?

Without any name?

9 79888 6411546